Simple Solutions®

Safety

By
Kim Campbell Thornton
Illustrations by Buck Jones

Plus Seasonal Advice

BOWTIE
P R E S S®

A Division of BowTie, Inc.
Laguna Hills, CA

Karla Austin, *Director of Operations and Product Development*
Nick Clemente, *Special Consultant*
Barbara Kimmel, *Editor in Chief*
Kara Smith, *Production Supervisor*
Heather Malk, *Layout Design*
Cover and book design concept by Michael V. Capozzi

The dogs in this book are referred to as *he* and *she* in alternating chapters.

Library of Congress Cataloging-in-Publication Data

Thornton, Kim Campbell.
 Safety / by Kim Campbell Thornton ; illustrations by Buck Jones.
   p. cm. — (Simple solutions)
 ISBN: 978-1-933958-25-5
1. Dogs—Safety measures. I. Jones, Buck. II. Title.

 SF427.T4926 2008
 636.7'0893—dc22
                          2007030958

BowTie Press®
A Division of BowTie, Inc.
23172 Plaza Pointe Dr., Ste. 230
Laguna Hills, CA 92653

Printed and bound in Singapore
13 12 11 10 09 08   1 2 3 4 5 6 7 8 9 10

Contents

Safety Begins at Home

It's said that most accidents occur in the home. That's true for pets as well. With their innate curiosity, desire to test everything for edibility, and super sense of smell, dogs fall prey to household accidents every day. They snarf up snail bait, gnaw on electrical cords, drink out of the toilet, eat socks and dish towels, and the list goes on.

Some dogs survive these incidents unscathed; others get an upset tummy. But occasionally a dog's exploratory forays result in much more serious consequences, from expensive emergency surgery to, sadly, death by electrocution, poisoning, or intestinal obstruction. With a little preparation, however, you can keep your dog—and your home and belongings—safe.

Dog proof your home *before* you bring home that new puppy or shelter adoptee, and you'll have fewer destructive incidents. It's never too late to start.

Start by getting down on your hands and knees. You want to look at every aspect of your house from a dog's-eye view. Think like a dog. Don't the cords underneath the desk look chewable? The cord hanging down from the mini blinds would be awfully fun to grab onto and pull. And if you paw at it enough, that bathroom cabinet door opens right up.

Once you've identified the dangers, you can put hazardous items and things you don't want broken or destroyed out of your dog's reach, make them unpalatable, or block them from her attentions. Here are some tips:

- Place trash up high—on top of the refrigerator or behind a latched cabinet.

- Put child locks on cabinets containing food, medications, or toxic substances such as cleansers or poisons.

- Use a spray-on unpalatable substance to prevent chewing on furniture (test it first to make sure it doesn't discolor anything).

- Put up baby gates to block access to forbidden areas.

- Keep shoes and dirty clothes behind closed closet doors.

- Place magazines, books, and treasured breakables out of reach.

When you're not able to supervise a lively dog, confine her to a crate or a room that's completely dog proofed, such as a bathroom or a laundry room.

Common Household Risks

When we think about dangers to pets in the home, we immediately think of two: electrocution from chewing on electrical cords and poisoning from ingesting toxic substances. Dogs, however, find countless creative ways to injure themselves. With a little forethought, though, you can prevent most such incidents.

That Daring Young Dog

Who doesn't know a dog that loves to jump up onto the sofa for a nice nap or simply to observe family goings-on from a high vantage point? Some breeds, such as the Japanese Chin and the Italian Greyhound, have been known to use furniture as a launching pad to reach even higher places in the home, such as fireplace mantels. You may think your dog isn't capable of reaching anything on the kitchen counter, but don't be surprised if one day you come home and find he's jumped from chair to table to counter, knocked a box of scone mix to the floor, and jumped back down to eat it. Tall breeds such as the Greyhound don't need to climb. They're well known for their counter-surfing abilities.

But landing badly—or simply placing too much stress on still developing bones and joints—can lead to strains, sprains, and broken bones. Tiny dogs with fragile bones are especially prone to fractures from jumping off furniture, but larger dogs can injure themselves as well.

Teach your dog from day one to use a set of steps to get on and off furniture. Pet steps are widely available at pet supply stores or through catalogs or online pet retailers. Consider rearranging furniture to deter acrobatic dogs from climbing to unsafe heights or reaching things they shouldn't. If you have slick hardwood or tile floors, lay down some area rugs—use

antiskid rug holders—to provide good footing and prevent your dog from slipping and sliding into a wall or a heavy piece of furniture.

Stairs are another safety hazard. A dog that's not used to them may tumble head over tail down them; a small dog could jump or fall through the railings on open stairways. Use a barricade until you're sure your dog can navigate stairs without incident.

Those Pesky Cords

Electrical cords and cords for window blinds pose a threat to dogs; both are found in almost every room of the home. Biting down on an electrical cord can give a dog a nasty shock or even kill him; getting tangled in window blind cords can choke or otherwise injure him.

To prevent electric shocks, unplug what you can. Cover cords with tough plastic cord covers, or run them through flexible plastic tubing (both are available at hardware stores). Wrap long cords up and place them out of reach. If you have a home computer, consider acquiring a wireless keyboard and a rechargeable cordless optical mouse to cut down on the number of cords in your home.

Products made of protective tubing work with phone cords, computer wires, and other household appliance cords, including

Christmas lights and audio/video connection cables. Some are citrus scented, which deters some dogs; it's also tough enough to withstand chewing, if need be.

Another option is to coat insulated cords with unpleasant substances. Try coating them with a foul-tasting spray or paste; smearing them with glue and then sprinkling on some cayenne pepper; coating them with Tabasco sauce, Mentholatum, or moistened bar soap; or wrapping them in aluminum foil, which most dogs don't like to bite down on

Window Cords

There are countless ways a dog can become entangled in blinds or other window coverings. His neck, collar, leg, paw, or tail can be caught in a dangling cords, which tightens as the dog tries to escape; his head can become wedged between the slats of blinds. He may even pull the curtains down

entirely, either in an attempt to get a better view or simply because the fabric looked fun to play with.

If your blinds or curtains have cords, consider cutting the cords to remove any loops that could entrap the dog. Alternatively, you could tape the cord up out of reach or attach a suction cup with a hook high on the window and loop the cord around that. Whenever possible, tie back curtains and keep vertical blinds pulled to one side.

Other Hazardous Items

What else might your dog get into? Think batteries, candy, cat litter boxes, tobacco products (including nicotine gum and patches), cleaning supplies, coins, dental floss, diaper pails, dirty laundry, jewelry, medicine bottles, mothballs, paper clips, pen caps, rodent poison, rubber bands, sewing kits, staples, thumbtacks, toilet bowl cleaners, toys, trash containers, yarn, string, and ribbon. These objects are choking hazards, and if your dog does manage to swallow them, they can damage her intestinal tract as they pass through. Pennies minted after 1982 contain high levels of zinc, which is toxic to dogs. Medication bottles or other containers that are childproof are not necessarily dog proof.

Whatever is accessible, your dog will investigate and probably try to eat. Your bottle of floor cleaner may be safely out of her reach, but if she walks across a freshly mopped floor and then licks her paws, she can ingest the solution that way.

Dangling dish towels, dirty socks, and pantyhose are favorite chew toys—dogs have been known to swallow them whole. Sometimes the items pass through, but often they cause intestinal obstructions that require expensive surgical repair. Plenty of dogs die from eating dish towels or other fabric items because the obstruction isn't discovered in time. Place dirty clothes in hampers behind closed closet doors, and keep dish towels out of reach.

Untreated toilet bowl water is not toxic. Nevertheless, keep your dog away from it; puppies have been known to fall into toilets and drown. Water that is treated with an automatic toilet bowl cleanser *is* toxic. Keep the toilet lid down.

While eating cat litter and kitty poop won't necessarily make your dog sick, you won't appreciate being licked by her afterward. Your dog can also acquire intestinal worms via cat poop. If your dog is larger than your cat, try placing the litter box behind a

pet door that only the cat fits through. Or block access to the box with a baby gate, and either raise the gate just high enough for the cat to slip under, or cut a hole in a bottom corner, big

enough to let the cat through but not the dog.

Think "up" and "out of sight" when deciding where to store things. Puppies love to crawl under things, but if you store an item where they can't see, smell, or reach it, it's probably safe.

Dining Dangers

It often seems as if dogs have cast-iron stomachs. The variety of objects they've been known to eat, seemingly without harm, is astounding. There are stories of dogs eating cell phones, rocks, and rotting seagulls with no ill effects! Nevertheless, many apparently harmless foods can make them deathly ill. Here are some to avoid:

Alcoholic beverages   Fatty foods
Avocado   Garlic
Chocolate (all forms)   Macadamia nuts
Coffee (all forms)   Moldy or spoiled foods

Onions and onion powder

Products sweetened with xylitol

Raisins and grapes

Salt

Tea

Yeast dough

What is the problem when it comes to these foods? It's that even though dogs' physiology is similar to ours, dogs react dif-

ferently to certain foods, intoxicants, and medications. Never assume that because something is OK for you to eat or drink, it must be safe for your dog as well.

Alcoholic beverages—beer, wine, and hard liquor—contain ethanol, which affects a dog's central nervous system and can depress the respiratory rate and cause cardiac arrest. It's particularly toxic to puppies, whose bodies aren't mature. Never leave alcoholic drinks within reach of your dog or give them to him on purpose. If your dog does down a daiquiri, waste no time getting him to the veterinarian or emergency clinic: he may need respiratory support or intravenous fluid therapy.

Chocolate, coffee, and tea contain caffeine and theobromine. These substances, called xanthines, can damage a dog's nervous system or urinary tract and cause reactions ranging from diarrhea and seizures to death. The darker the chocolate is, the more serious the toxicity. Take your dog to the vet or emergency clinic if he's raided the Halloween stash or eaten a chocolate Easter bunny; and keep fudge, chocolate chips, and Valentine's gifts well out of reach.

Fatty or salty foods such as ham or the fat trimmed from a steak can lead to vomiting and diarrhea or pancreatitis—a painful inflammation of the pancreas that's sometimes fatal.

Give your dog healthier snacks: lean chicken or turkey, apple slices, or raw baby carrots.

Onions, garlic, chives, and onion products such as onion powder contain an active ingredient that damages red blood cells, causing a condition known as Heinz body anemia. The falling number of red blood cells causes pale mucous membranes, depression, increased heart and respiratory rate, kidney damage, weakness, fever, and loss of appetite. If your dog snatches an onion-laden burger or eats an onion slice that's dropped to the floor, take him to your vet. And if you're using baby foods to entice your dog

to eat, check the labels first: some baby foods contain onion salt.

Don't let your dog dip into the guacamole. Its main ingredient is avocado, which is high in fat and can cause vomiting and diarrhea in dogs that eat large amounts.

Next time you have a luau, no tossing macadamia nuts to your dog! They can cause weakness, depression, vomiting, tremors, and increased body temperature. Signs usually develop in less than 12 hours. Call your veterinarian for advice if your dog nabs some of these nuts, especially if they're chocolate covered.

Yeast dough expands in the stomach and can block or rupture the intestines. Place rising dough where your dog can't get to it.

Grapes and raisins can cause kidney failure in dogs. Don't give any whatsoever to your dog.

Some sugar-free chewing gums, candies, and baked goods contain a sweetener called xylitol, which can be toxic or even life threatening to dogs. Dogs that eat such products can suffer a sudden drop in blood sugar, causing depression, loss of coordination, and seizures. These signs can occur as little as half an hour or as long as twelve hours after ingestion. There may also be a link between xylitol ingestion and liver failure in

dogs. Call your vet if your dog eats anything containing xylitol, or contact the Animal Poison Control Center run by the American Society for the Prevention of Cruelty to Animals (ASPCA). (A consulting fee applies.)

Needless to say, if food is moldy or spoiled, your dog shouldn't eat it. Toss it into your secured, dog-proofed trash can, along with coffee grounds, poultry bones, packaging for meat, meat trimmings, and the string from that roast.

Plant Precautions

Despite being carnivores, dogs can be determined in their attempts to munch on plants. They like to nibble grass and pluck ripe berries from bushes. They'll dig up bulbs—that turned-up dirt smells so good!—and of course, check plants to see if they're edible. Unfortunately, the super-powerful canine sense of smell doesn't include a poison detector, so it's not uncommon for dogs to get sick or even die from eating toxic plants.

In some cases, only certain parts of a plant are toxic; in others, all parts are poisonous. Don't take any chances.

Remove the following plants from your home and yard, or see that your dog doesn't have access to them: azalea/rhododendron, castor bean, cyclamen, kalanchoe, lilies, marijuana, oleander,  sago palm, tulip and narcissus bulbs, and yew.

Common signs of plant poisoning include vomiting, drooling, diarrhea, weakness, abdominal pain, excessive thirst, loss of appetite, depression, incoordination, and seizures. Plant toxins can damage the heart, liver, and kidneys; severe cases can lead to coma and even death.

Certain plants associated with the holidays are toxic. Easter lilies are highly toxic, as are holly and mistletoe berries when consumed in large amounts. Poinsettias contain a sap that can irritate the mouth. Celebrate the holidays with beautiful *artificial* plants, and share the holiday spirit by passing on gifts of live toxic plants to people without pets.

The plants discussed above are just a few of many with toxic effects. More are listed below, but any time you're not sure, call a local nursery, or ask your veterinarian for advice.

Indoor Plants

Amaryllis
Asparagus fern
Bird of paradise
Boston ivy
Caladium
Chrysanthemum
Creeping fig

Dieffenbachia
  (dumb cane)
Elephant's ear
Jack-in-the-pulpit
Jerusalem cherry
Mother-in-law
plant

Nightshade
Philodendron
Pothos
Pot mum
Spider mum
Tuberous begonia
Umbrella plant

Outdoor Plants

Angel's trumpet
Buttercup
Chinaberry
Daffodil
Delphinium
Foxglove
Indian tobacco
Jasmine

Jimsonweed
Locoweed
Lupine
May apple
Monkey pod
Morning glory
Mushrooms
Periwinkle

Pokeweed
Rain tree
Rhubarb
Tomato vine
Water hemlock
Wisteria

Yard Safety

Poet Robert Frost once wrote that "good fences make good neighbors." Breeders and animal shelters believe that good fences make good dog owners, too, and often refuse to let dogs go to adoptive homes that have no fenced yard. There's more to yard safety than just having a fence, though. The type of fence, the condition it's in, gate security, pools, spas, the presence of mulch and compost, and the use of pesticides and herbicides are all factors to consider.

Fences and Gates

Solid wood or masonry fences six feet high or more are best for containing dogs and preventing "fence fighting," the barking and snarling that often occur when dogs see people or other animals passing by their property. Tough chain-link fences keep dogs in but give them a view of all passersby. Post-and-rail fences keep large dogs contained, but smaller dogs can slip beneath them or wriggle through the spaces between the rails.

Whatever type of fence you have, make sure it's in good repair. Do a regular fence check for holes or loose planks that could facilitate an escape or sharp edges that could cause injury.

Avoid placing picnic tables, doghouses, or other potential launching pads too near the fence.

Check gates for safety as well. They should latch securely without being forced. Some decorative wrought iron gates have spaces large enough for dogs to wriggle through. Block them with chicken wire or a section from a portable exercise pen, available from a pet supply store.

Pools, Spas, and Ponds

Bodies of water are just as dangerous to dogs as they are to toddlers. It's often assumed that every dog can dog paddle, but dogs don't naturally know how to swim. Some dogs can't swim at all. Bulldogs, for instance, are so top-heavy that they're unable to stay afloat.

Protect your dog from drowning by preventing access to the pool, spa, or koi pond unless you're there to supervise. Let your novice swimmer get his paws wet gradually. Throw a toy into the shallow end to encourage your dog into the water, and be ready to help if he starts flail-

ing when he realizes he's not touching bottom. Don't let him go very far until he's comfortable in the water. Rinse your dog's coat thoroughly after every swim so his fur doesn't become damaged and dry from the pool chemicals.

Even if your dog isn't a swimmer, he should know how and where to get in and out of the pool, just in case he falls in. Take him into the pool using the steps, and let him practice going in and out until he can do it on his own. Some companies make ramps that are easily visible and can be placed anywhere in the pool.

Other Garden Hazards

The aroma from the compost heap may be tempting to your dog, but it's definitely not something you want him rolling in or eating. Compost is, after all, decaying material. The bacteria in it can cause vomiting and seizures, so store compost in a dog-proof container.

Coffee grounds are toxic, and mulch made from cocoa bean shells can cause signs of illness similar to those of chocolate toxicosis. According to a 2003 study of six dogs whose poisoning cases were managed by the ASPCA's poison control center, dogs that ate cocoa mulch suffered vomiting and muscle tremors, with severity increasing the more the dog ate. Other signs were elevated heart rates, hyperactivity, and diarrhea. Avoid using

cocoa mulch in areas to which your dog has access. If you discover that he has eaten a significant amount of cocoa mulch, contact your veterinarian or the ASPCA's poison control center.

Beautiful yards and dogs can go together, but it's important to take care with fertilizers and pesticides, especially ant and snail bait; both are deadly to dogs. If you must use pesticides, choose those that contain low-residue pyrethrins rather than the more toxic organophosphates. Look into natural insect repellents, such as marigolds, tansies, nasturtiums, and ladybugs. When applying pesticides or fertilizers, restrict your dog's access to the treated area for at least 24 hours, and don't let her nibble on or roll in the grass. Bone meal fertilizer can cause gastrointestinal upset if eaten. Be aware, too, that bone meal, blood meal, and fish emulsion have a scent that

attracts dogs. Your dog may even dig up the area to get at the source of that attractive aroma!

Last but not least, take care in your placement of ornamental containers, fountains, and statues. They're easily knocked over by rambunctious dogs. Make sure they're well secured.

Seasonal Safety

Different times of the year present different dangers to dogs. Here's what you need to know to prevent seasonal problems.

Summer

Bees, wasps, fire ants, and mosquitoes are pernicious pests of summer. A bee or wasp sting can raise reactions from slight swelling and pain to anaphylaxis, a sudden, severe allergic reaction that can be fatal if not treated immediately. The synchronous sting of fire ants on a tender canine belly is exquisitely painful. Mosquito bites don't provoke a skin reaction, but they can transmit fatal heartworm disease. Warm weather also causes fleas to hatch. Many dogs are allergic to fleas, and a single flea bite can drive them into a frenzy of itching and scratching.

If a bee or wasp stings your dog, especially on the nose or head, seek veterinary assistance. Severe swelling in the head area can close off your dog's throat, making him unable to breathe. Prevent heartworm disease by giving a monthly chewable medication. Topical flea treatments can kill fleas for as long as a month. Some flea-control medications repel mosquitoes also, but they won't prevent heartworm disease.

Summer heat and humidity affects dogs, especially dogs with heavy coats and flat-faced breeds such as Bulldogs, Pugs, and Pekingese. Dogs kept outside or enclosed in cars are most at risk of heatstroke. Signs of heat exhaustion and heatstroke include excessive panting, fatigue, dizziness, nausea, and loss of consciousness. Cool a pet that has heat exhaustion by pouring lukewarm, not cold, water on the coat and working it into the hair. Loss of conscious-

ness is an emergency that requires immediate veterinary care.

Leave your dog in air-conditioned comfort during the day. If she must stay outside, give her plenty of cool, fresh water and a shady place to rest. Walk her during cool mornings and evenings.

Apply sunscreen to your dog's ears, nose, and belly if she enjoys lying in the sun, especially if her coat is thin or light colored. Dogs can get sunburned, and they are susceptible to skin cancer.

Most important, never leave your dog in a car during warm months. The temperature inside a car can climb to more than 120 degrees Fahrenheit in less than 10 minutes.

Winter

Common concerns during winter are frostbite and toxicity from antifreeze and from a variety of de-icing products. Antifreeze has a sweet taste that dogs like, but its primary ingredient, ethylene glycol, is highly toxic. As little as two

ounces can be fatal. Clean up antifreeze spills immediately, and watch for coolant leaks in your garage or driveway. Never leave an open container of antifreeze where your dog could reach it.

Holidays

Christmas trees, brightly wrapped packages, stockings, and tinsel—dogs find these irresistible and can destroy a perfectly decorated 12-foot blue spruce before you know it. Toxic plants, chocolate, and rich foods are another recipe for disaster.

Protect your tree from your dog—and vice versa—with a lightly electrified mat. It encircles the tree, and when your dog sets paw on it, she receives the equivalent of a carpet shock to stop her in her tracks. This is especially important if you have a live tree. The water keeping the tree fresh contains chemicals that are toxic to dogs, so keep your dog from slurping it.

Avoid a trip to the emergency room by disposing of twine used to tie up the turkey or roast and placing packages tied with yarn or ribbons well out of reach. Too late? Once string or tinsel is down the throat, don't try to pull it out—you could severely damage your dog's insides. Take her to the veterinarian immediately.

Keep snow globes out of reach. The liquid inside contains antifreeze, so place them out of your dog's reach.

Decorate your tree with beautiful, nontoxic, unbreakable objects. Substitute baby's breath, for example, for tinsel, which can cause intestinal blockages if swallowed.

Treat Christmas lights with Bitter Apple spray. Pets that bite bulbs can be electrocuted or require reconstructive surgery because of burns to the mouth.

Anchor your tree to the wall or ceiling with fishing line.

Keeping your dog safe is mainly a matter of being prepared. Know the phone numbers for your veterinarian and the

ASPCA's Animal Poison Control Center (888-426-4435). Keep a record of your dog's weight and any medications she takes—useful information if emergency treatment is needed. And if your dog has eaten something toxic, bring the label with you to the vet or know the scientific name of the plant she ate.

It may seem as if your home is full of hazards, but with a little forethought and preparation, you can keep it safe for—and from—your dog.

Kim Campbell Thornton is an award-winning writer and editor. During her tenure as editor of *Dog Fancy,* the magazine won three Dog Writers Association of America Maxwell Awards for best all-breed magazine. Her book *Why Do Cats Do That?* was named best behavior book in 1997 by the Cat Writers' Association. Kim is the author of the Simple Solutions series books *Aggression, Barking, Chewing, Digging,* and *House-Training.* She serves on the DWAA Board of Governors and on the board of the Dog Writers Educational Trust.

Buck Jones's humorous illustrations have appeared in numerous magazines (including *Dog Fancy* and *Cat Fancy*) and books. He is the illustrator for the best-selling Simple Solutions series books; *Why Do Cockatiels Do That?*; *Why Do Parakeets Do That?*; *Kittens! Why Do They Do What They Do?*; and *Puppies! Why Do They Do What They Do?* Contact Buck through his Web site: http://www.buckjonesillustrator.com.